UNOFFICIAL HOW TO DRAW FORTNITE

LEARN TO DRAW SKINS

COPYRIGHT © OSIE PUBLISHING

THIS BOOK IS NO WAY AUTHORIZED, ENDORSED OR AFFILIATED WITH FORTNITE OR EPIC GAMES. ALL FORTNITE REFERENCES ARE USED IN ACCORDANCE WITH THE FAIR USE OF DOCTRINE AND ARE NOT MEANT TO IMPLY THAT THIS BOOK IS A FORTNITE PRODUCT FOR ADVERTISING OR OTHER COMMERCIAL PURPOSES. ALL ASPECTS OF THE GAME INCLUDING CHARACTERS, THEIR NAMES, LOCATIONS, AND OTHER FEATURES OF THE GAME WITHIN BOOK ARE TRADEMARKED AND OWNED BY THEIR RESPECTIVE OWNERS.

CONNECT US :

#OSIEPUBLISHING

THIS BOOK BELONGS TO:

DEFAULT OUTFIT

DEFAULT OUTFIT

(1) Draw hers head with
ears, rather long chin
and spiky hairstyle.

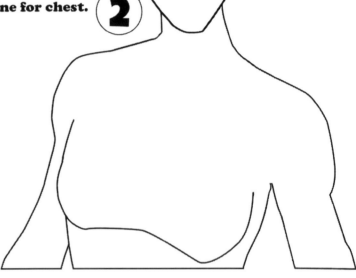

Continue with hers neck, arms
and a line for chest. **(2)**

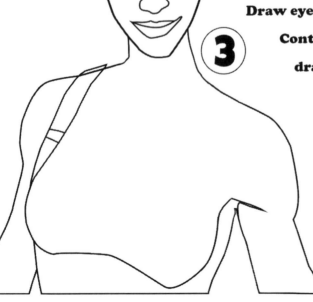

Draw eyes, eyebrows, nose and lips.
Continue hers chestline to
draw armpit and lace. **(3)**

DEFAULT OUTFIT

4 Draw the other lace and armband.

5 Then draw dog tags.

6 Finally, delete all unnecessary lines to merge the body.

HIGHRISE ASSAULT TROOPER

HIGHRISE ASSULT TROOPER

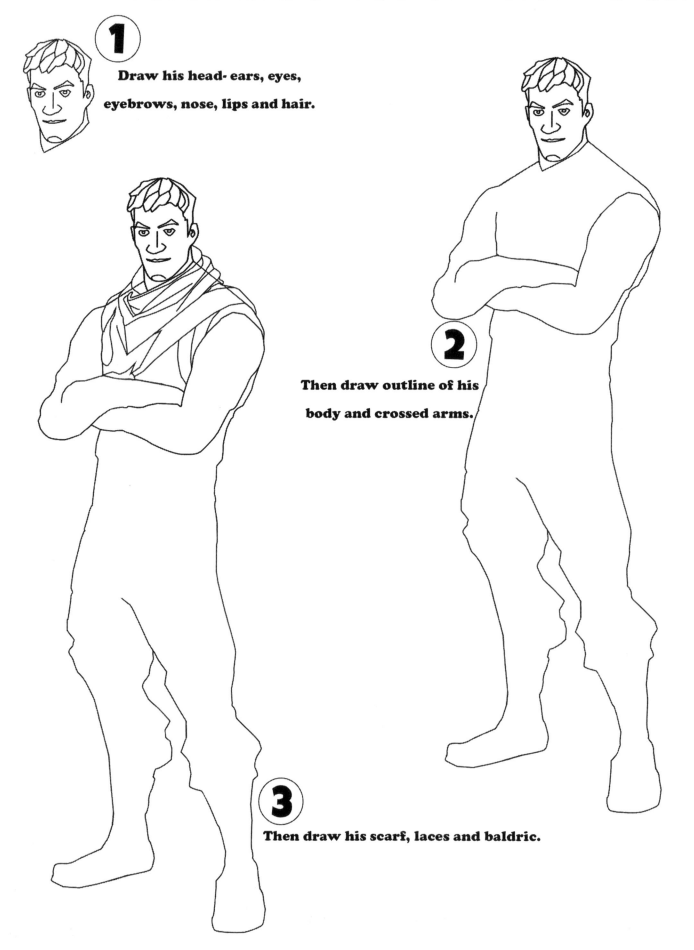

1 Draw his head- ears, eyes, eyebrows, nose, lips and hair.

2 Then draw outline of his body and crossed arms.

3 Then draw his scarf, laces and baldric.

HIGHRISE ASSULT TROOPER

4 Then draw belt and shin guards.

5 Draw his watch, glowes, second belt, pockets and boots.

Finally, delete all unnecessary lines to merge the body. **6**

PATHFINDER

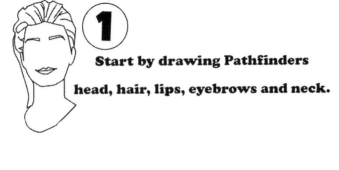

1

Start by drawing Pathfinders

head, hair, lips, eyebrows and neck.

2

Then draw hers body outline with

arms and legs. Add a line to hers chest.

3 Draw eyes and nose to her face.

Draw laces, armband, watch and dog tags.

4 Then draw gloves, belt straps on leg and knee pad on left knee.

PATHFINDER

5 Draw her boots and shin pad.

Finally, delete all unnecessary lines to merge the body. **6**

DESPERADO

DESPERADO

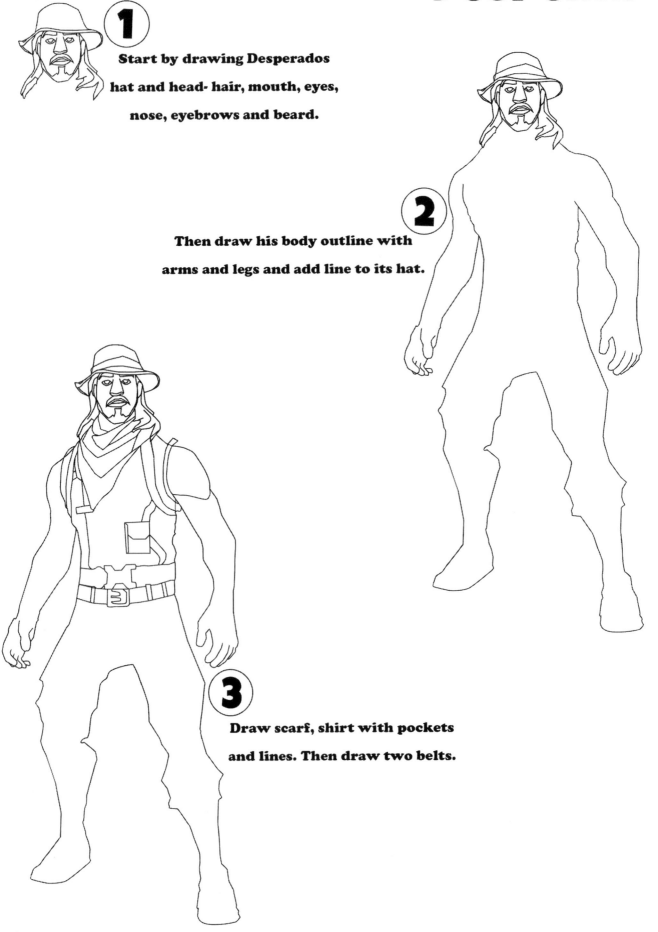

1 Start by drawing Desperados hat and head- hair, mouth, eyes, nose, eyebrows and beard.

2 Then draw his body outline with arms and legs and add line to its hat.

3 Draw scarf, shirt with pockets and lines. Then draw two belts.

DESPERADO

4 Then draw shin pads and boots.

5 Draw his pockets, arm band, gloves and baldric. Add lines to pants.

6 Finally, delete all unnecessary lines to merge the body.

RABBIT RAIDER

RABBIT RAIDER

1 Start by drawing Rabbit Raiders head- face with mask, mouth, nose and eyes.

2 Then draw his body with crossed arms and boots.

3 Add dots and lines to its mask. Add lines to its body and small ears to its boots. Add to its hood.

RABBIT RAIDER

4 Then draw baldric with attached grenades and a small bag on its upper leg. Add to its pants.

5 Draw his bag that look like an easter egg.

Finally, add to boots. Delete all unnecessary lines to merge the body. **6**

FIREWORKS TEAM LEADER

FIREWORKS TEAM LEADER

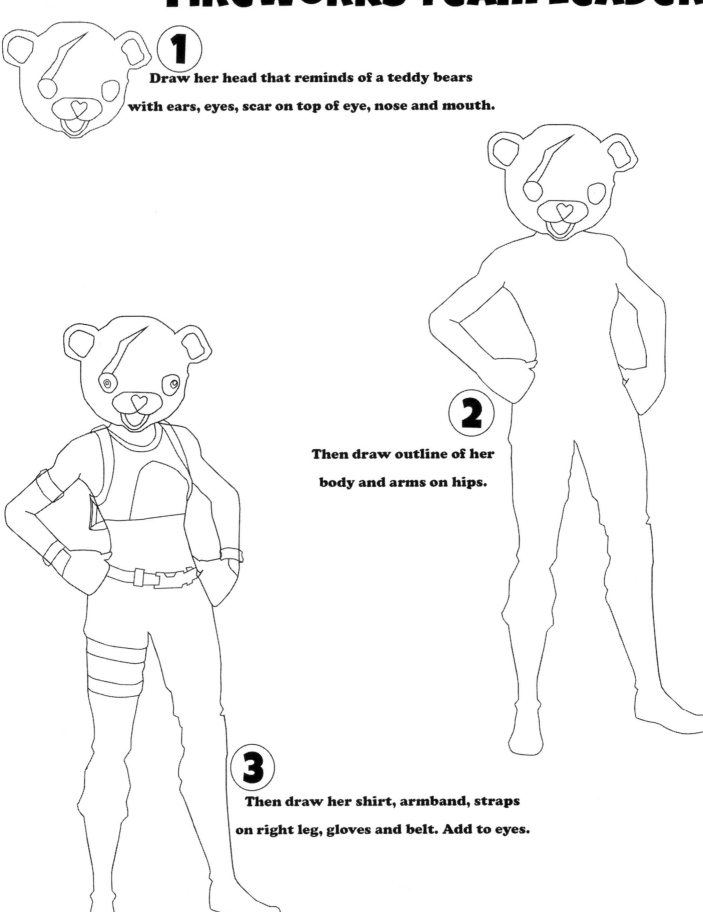

1 Draw her head that reminds of a teddy bears with ears, eyes, scar on top of eye, nose and mouth.

2 Then draw outline of her body and arms on hips.

3 Then draw her shirt, armband, straps on right leg, gloves and belt. Add to eyes.

FIREWORKS TEAM LEADER

4 Then draw shin guard, knee pad and shoelaces. Add lines to her body.

5 Draw her watch, soles to boots and rockets behind her right shoulder.

6 Finally, delete all unnecessary lines to merge the body.

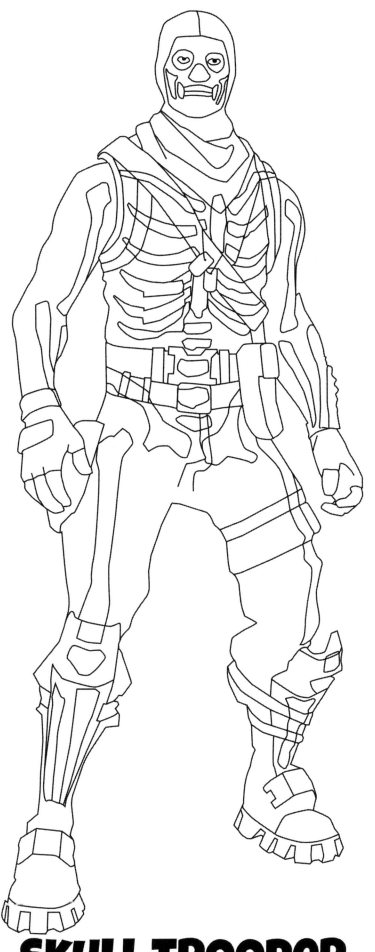

SKULL TROOPER

SKULL TROOPER

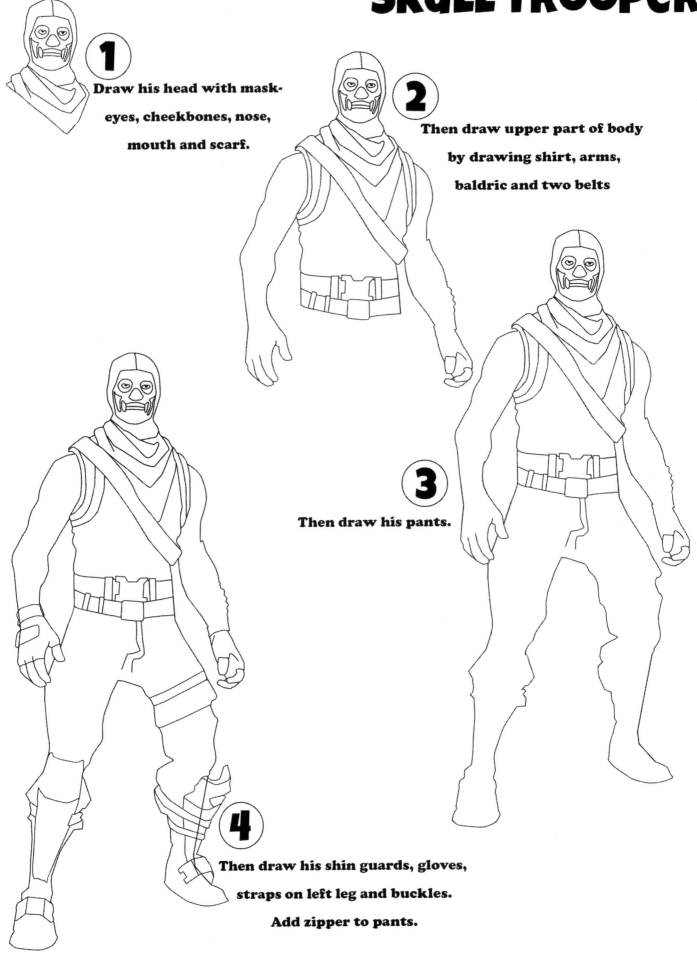

1 Draw his head with mask- eyes, cheekbones, nose, mouth and scarf.

2 Then draw upper part of body by drawing shirt, arms, baldric and two belts

3 Then draw his pants.

4 Then draw his shin guards, gloves, straps on left leg and buckles. Add zipper to pants.

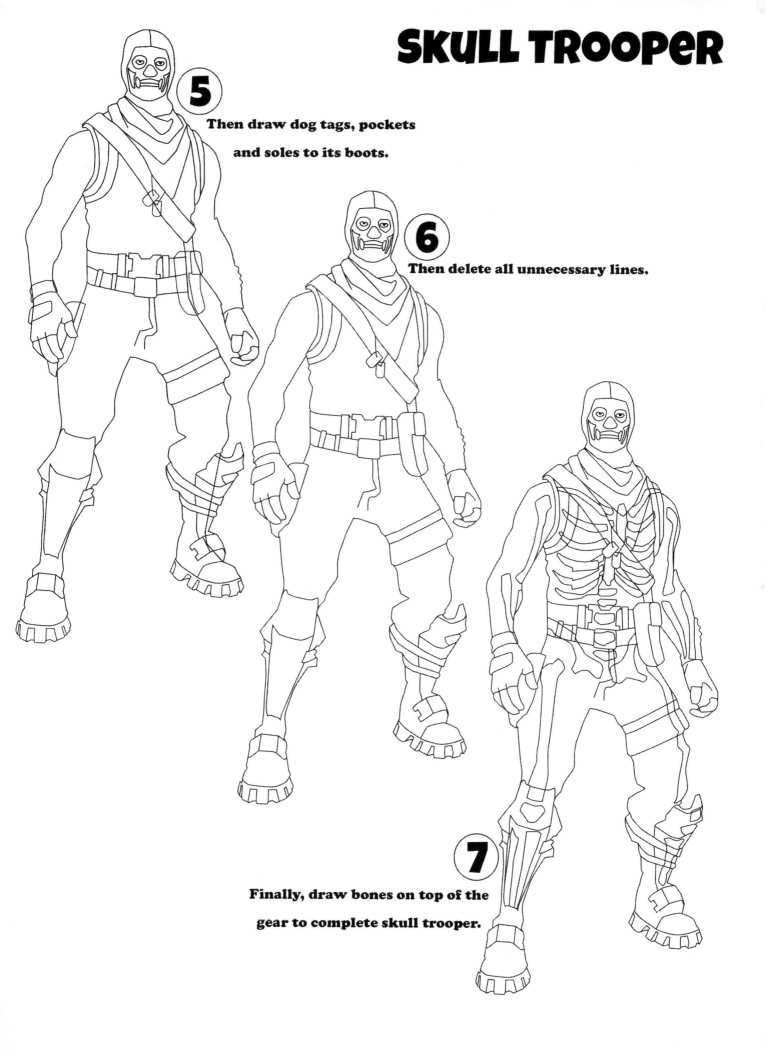

SKULL TROOPER

5

Then draw dog tags, pockets and soles to its boots.

6

Then delete all unnecessary lines.

7

Finally, draw bones on top of the gear to complete skull trooper.

DRIFT

DRIFT

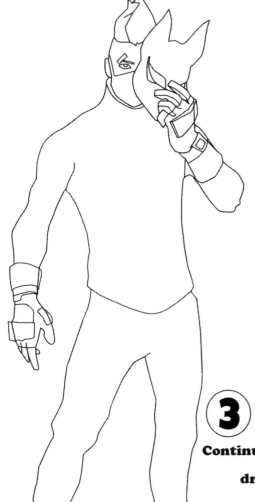

1 Start by drawing Drifts
head with spiky hairstyle and
a hand with mask in it.

2 Then draw his body outline with arms
and legs. Add line to divide its shirt from pants.

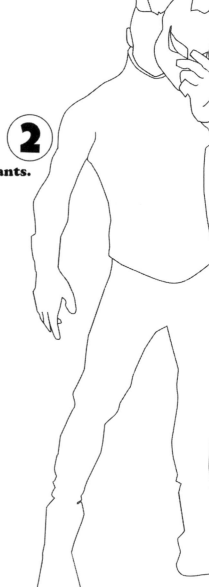

3 Continue with his face,
draw gloves.

4 Then finalize his mask.

5 Draw his shirt, boots and shorts with large pockets.

6 Finally, delete all unnecessary lines to merge the body.

CRACKSHOT

CRACKSHOT

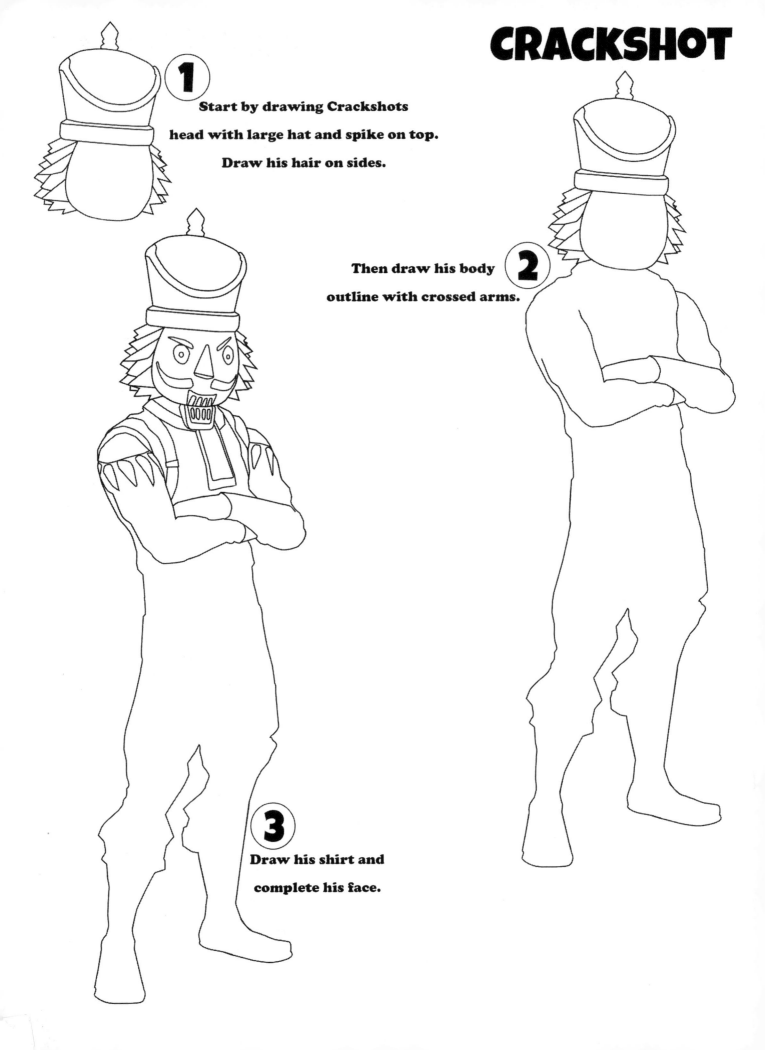

1 Start by drawing Crackshots head with large hat and spike on top. Draw his hair on sides.

2 Then draw his body outline with crossed arms.

3 Draw his shirt and complete his face.

CRACKSHOT

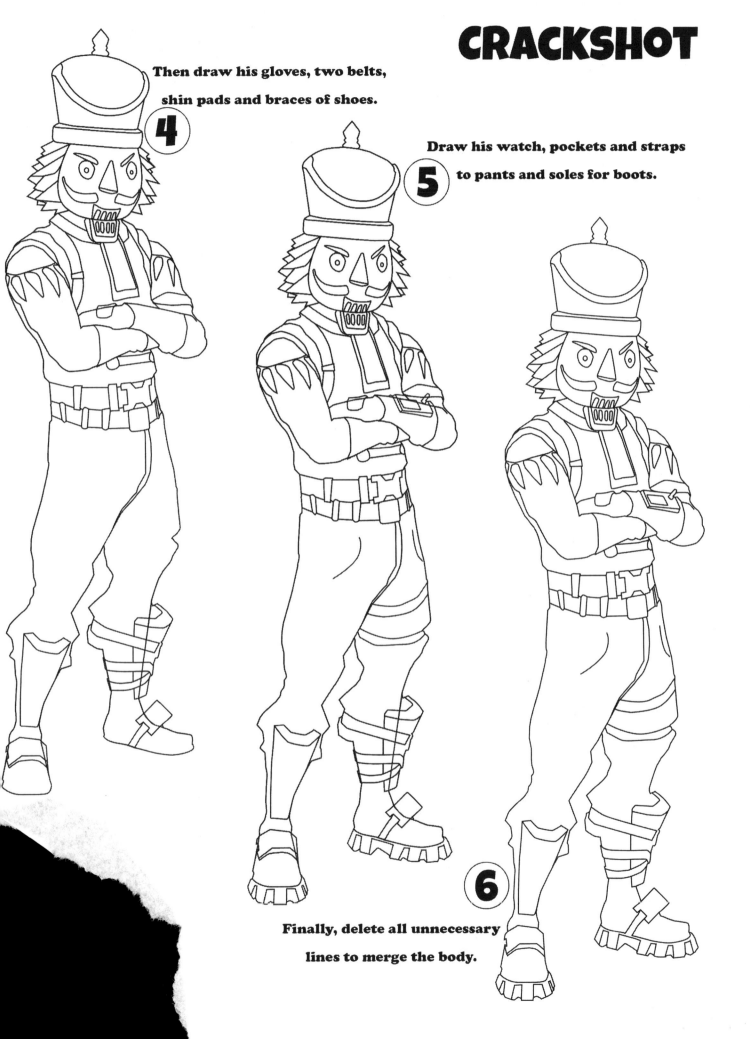

Then draw his gloves, two belts, shin pads and braces of shoes.

4

Draw his watch, pockets and straps to pants and soles for boots.

5

6

Finally, delete all unnecessary lines to merge the body.

CUDDLE TEAM LEADER

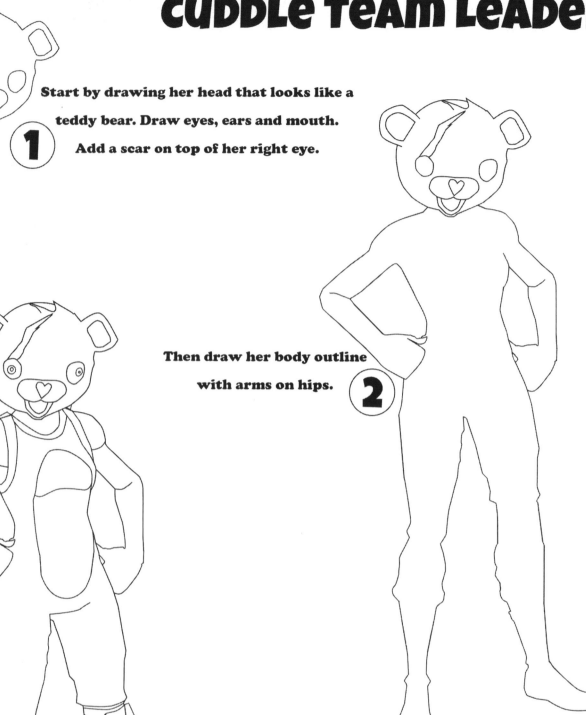

Start by drawing her head that looks like a teddy bear. Draw eyes, ears and mouth. Add a scar on top of her right eye.

1

Then draw her body outline with arms on hips.

2

Draw shirt with oval on her chest, add to arms and eyes. Draw knee pad on left knee.

3

CUDDLE TEAM LEADER

4 Then draw shin pads, shoelaces, straps on right leg, armband, watch and belt.

5 Draw broken heart on her tummy, soles for boots and bow on her back

6 Finally, delete all unnecessary lines to merge the body.

CODENAME E.L.F.

CODENAME E.L.F.

1 Start by drawing Elfs head with hair and hat on top. Draw his nose and mouth.

2 Then draw his body outline with crossed arms.

3 Draw scarf, elfs shirt and gloves. Finalize his face.

CODENAME E.L.F.

Then draw shin pads and braces for boots and straps on left leg.

4

Draw his two belts and watch.

Draw his soles for boots.

5

6

Finally, delete all unnecessary lines to merge the body.

THE REAPER

THE REAPER

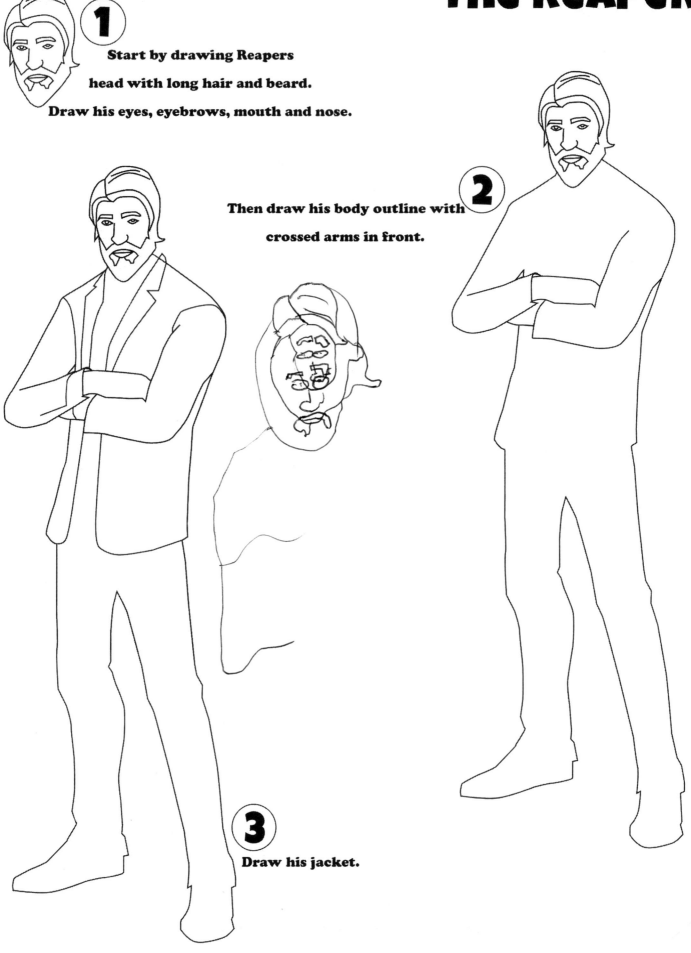

1 Start by drawing Reapers head with long hair and beard. Draw his eyes, eyebrows, mouth and nose.

Then draw his body outline with crossed arms in front. **2**

3 Draw his jacket.

THE REAPER

4 Then draw vest, shirt and tie.

Add lines to his pants.

Add to his jacket and vest pockets and

buttons. Draw soles to his shoes.

5

6 Finally, delete all

unnecessary lines to merge the body.

ROYALE KNIGHT

ROYALE KNIGHT

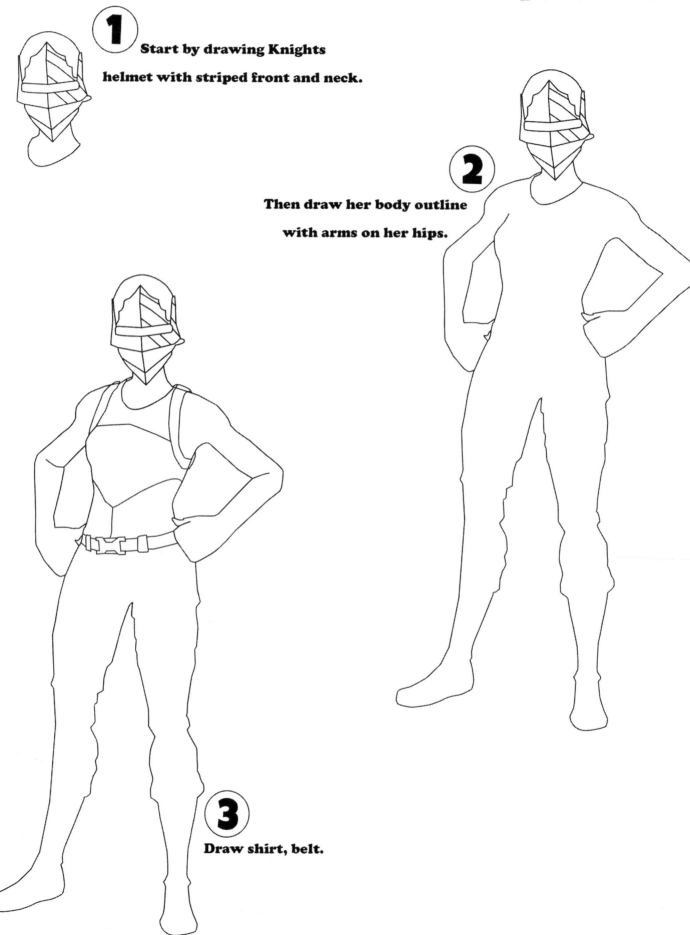

1 Start by drawing Knights helmet with striped front and neck.

2 Then draw her body outline with arms on her hips.

3 Draw shirt, belt.

ROYALE KNIGHT

4 Then draw shin and knee pad. Draw armband and gloves and straps on leg. Finalize shirt.

5 Draw her shield on back and watch. Finalize her boots.

6 Finally, delete all unnecessary lines to merge the body.

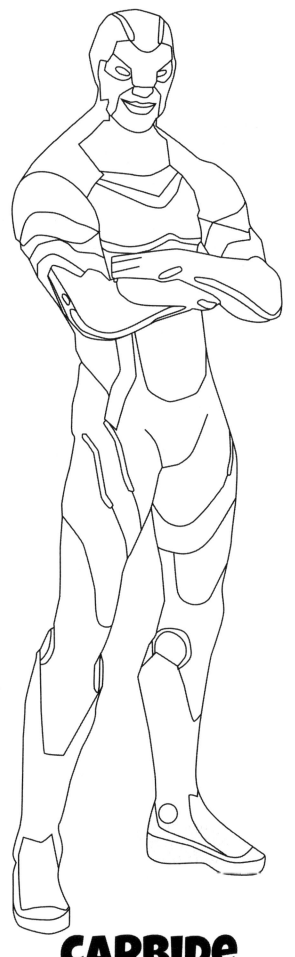

CARBIDE

CARBIDE

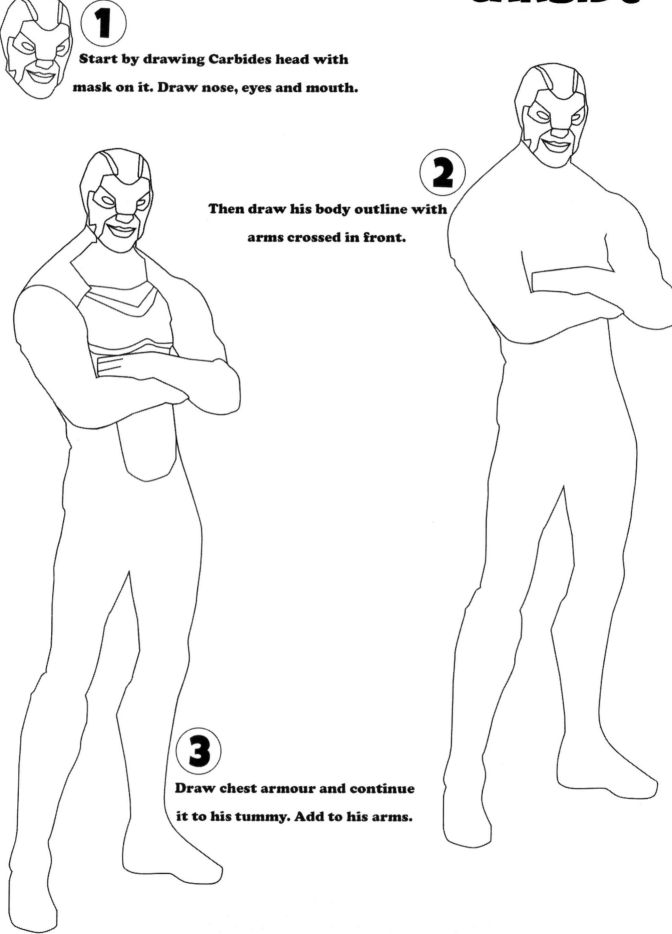

1 Start by drawing Carbides head with mask on it. Draw nose, eyes and mouth.

2 Then draw his body outline with arms crossed in front.

3 Draw chest armour and continue it to his tummy. Add to his arms.

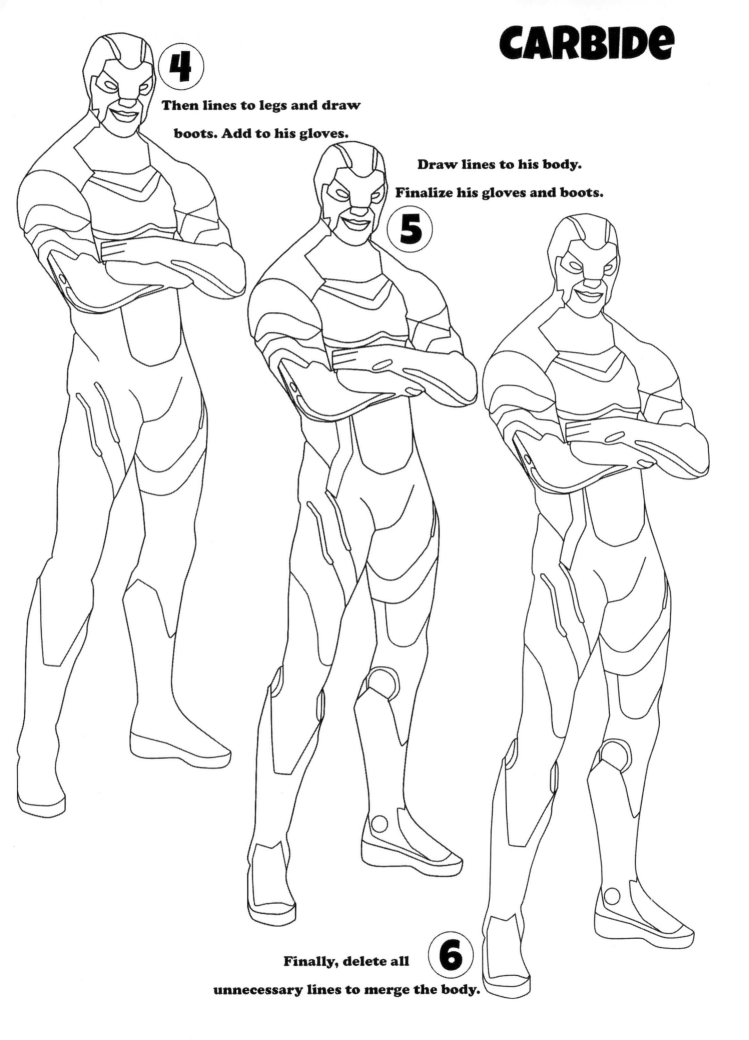

CARBIDE

4 Then lines to legs and draw boots. Add to his gloves.

Draw lines to his body.
Finalize his gloves and boots. **5**

Finally, delete all **6** unnecessary lines to merge the body.

WARPAINT

WARPAINT

1 Start by drawing Warpaints

hat and head- ears, mouth, eyes, nose.

Draw skeleton alike line on his face

2 Then draw his body outline

with arms and legs.

3 Draw scarf, shirt, baldric.

Draw his belt and add to arms.

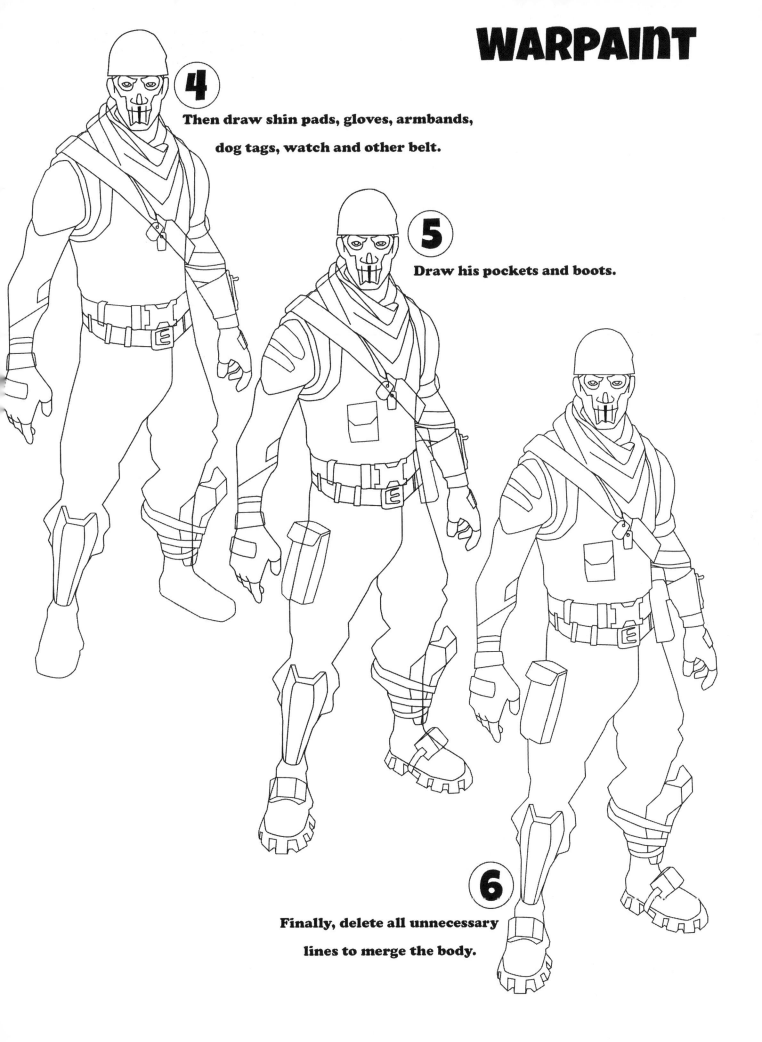

WARPAINT

4 Then draw shin pads, gloves, armbands, dog tags, watch and other belt.

5 Draw his pockets and boots.

6 Finally, delete all unnecessary lines to merge the body.

SKY STALKER

① Start by drawing Sky Stalkers gas mask and his hair on top.

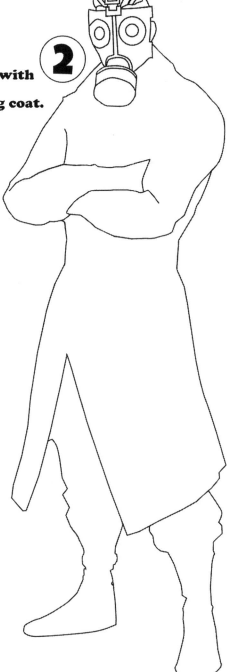

② Then draw his body outline with arms crossed in front and long coat.

③ Draw upper part of coat, gloves and soles for his boots.

SKY STALKER

4 Then draw belt, finalize his boots and draw oxygen tank on his back.

5 Finalize his gas mask and coat. Draw binoculars under right arm.

6 Finally, delete all unnecessary lines to merge the body.

omen

omen

1

Start by drawing Omens
face with mask and hood.

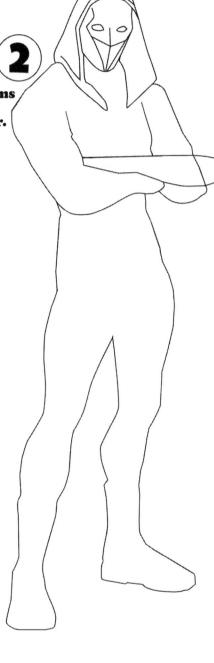

2

Then draw his body outline with arms
crossed in front and an arm armour.

3

Draw other arm armour, gloves
and armour on chest.

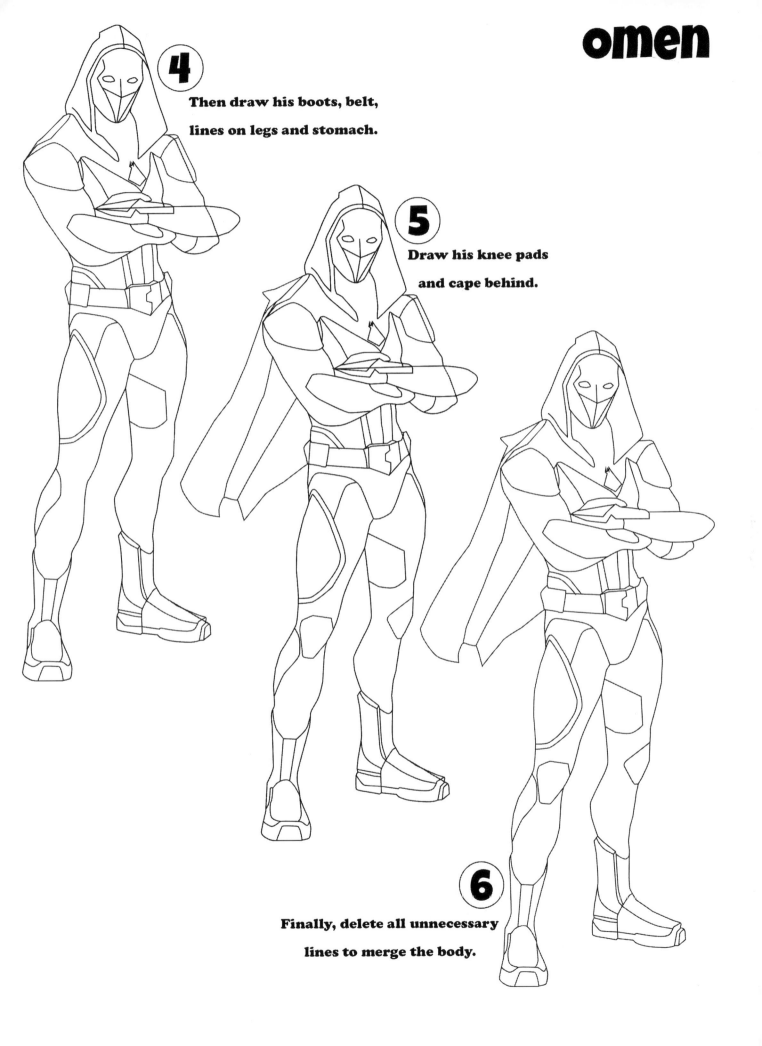

omen

4 Then draw his boots, belt, lines on legs and stomach.

5 Draw his knee pads and cape behind.

6 Finally, delete all unnecessary lines to merge the body.

DARK VOYAGER

DARK VOYAGER

Start by drawing Dark Voyagers
cosmonauts alike helmet.

1

2 Then draw his body outline with
his arms crossed in front.
Draw his right glove.

3 Draw right glove, zipper on stomach
and add to his trousers. Draw marking
on his shoulder and shoulder-straps.

RED KNIGHT

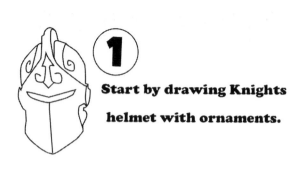

RED KNIGHT

1 Start by drawing Knights helmet with ornaments.

2 Then draw his body outline with her arms on hips.

3 Draw her shirt, watch and strap for glove on left arm and strap on left leg.

RED KNIGHT

4 Then draw shin pads, armband and belt. Add to boots and shirt.
Draw strap of glove to right arm and other strap on leg.

Draw her shield on back and knee pad. Draw soles of boots. **5**

Finally, delete all unnecessary lines to merge the body. **6**

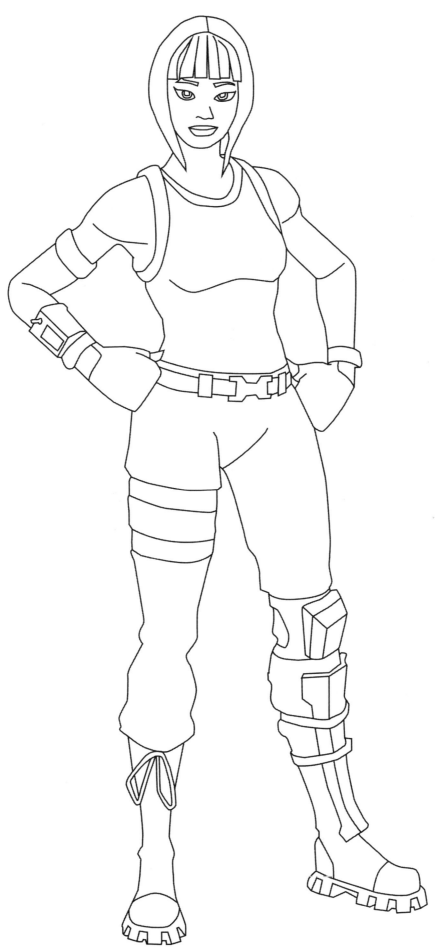

BRILLIANT STRIKER

BRILLIANT STRIKER

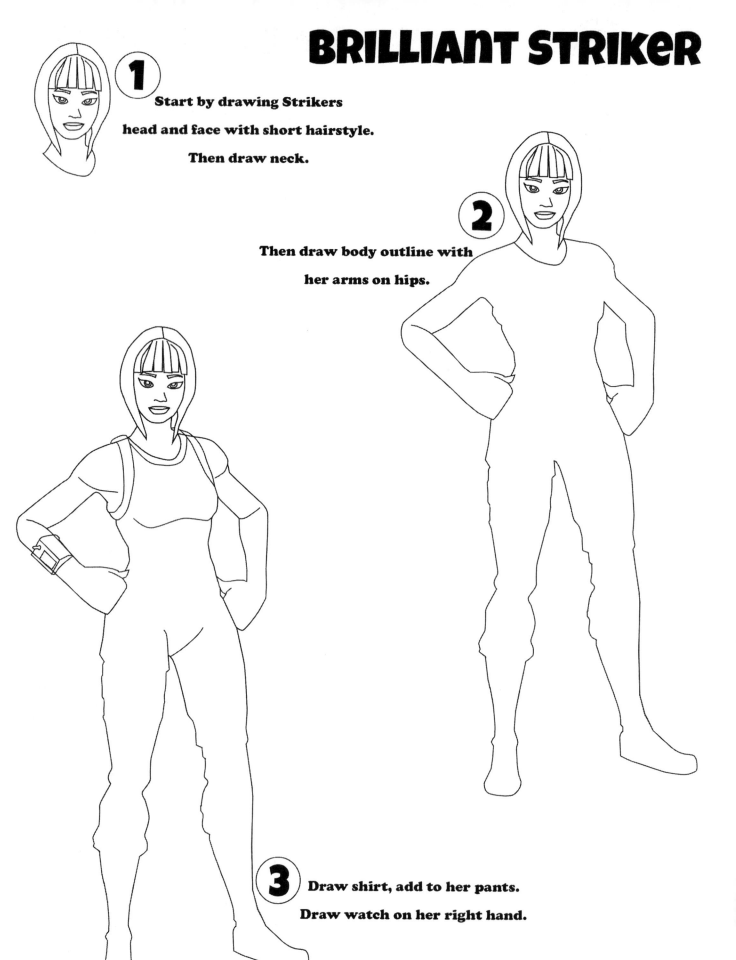

1 Start by drawing Strikers head and face with short hairstyle. Then draw neck.

2 Then draw body outline with her arms on hips.

3 Draw shirt, add to her pants. Draw watch on her right hand.

BRILLIANT STRIKER

Draw her knee pad and boots.

5

4 Then draw armband, gloves,
straps on leg, belt,
chestline, shin pads and shoelaces.

6 Finally, delete all unnecessary
lines to merge the body.

Printed in Great Britain
by Amazon